This book belongs to ...

....

OXFORD
UNIVERSITY PRESS

Great Clarendon Street, Oxford, OX2 6DP, United Kingdom

Oxford University Press is a department of the University of Oxford.
It furthers the University's objective of excellence in research, scholarship and
education by publishing worldwide. Oxford is a registered trade mark of Oxford
University Press in the UK and in certain other countries

Jack and the Beanstalk Text © Oxford University Press 2011
Illustrations © Constanze von Kitzing
The Moon in the Pond Text © Chris Powling 2011
Illustrations © Jeannie Winston
The Magic Paintbrush Text © Oxford University Press 2011
Illustrations © Meilo So
Oh, Jack! Text © Jan Burchett and Sara Vogler 2011
Illustrations © Teresa Murfin

The moral rights of the authors have been asserted

Jack and the Beanstalk, The Moon in the Pond, The Magic Paintbrush, Oh, Jack!
first published in 2011

This edition published in 2014

British Library Cataloguing in Publication Data
Data available

ISBN: 978-0-19-273607-9

10 9 8 7 6 5 4 3 2 1

Typeset in OUP Earlybird

Printed in China

Paper used in the production of this book is a natural, recyclable product
made from wood grown in sustainable forests. The manufacturing process
conforms to the environmental regulations of the country of origin.

Acknowledgements

Series Advisor: Nikki Gamble

Help your child's learning
with essential tips, phonics
support and free eBooks
www.oxfordowl.co.uk

Oxford
Reading
Tree

Jack and the Beanstalk

and Other Stories

OXFORD
UNIVERSITY PRESS

Tips for reading Jack and the Beanstalk together

About the story

This story is a simple retelling of the English folk tale, 'Jack and the Beanstalk'.

This book practises these sounds:

ay (as in 'day')   **g** (as in 'giantess')   **al** (as in 'beanstalk')

Ask your child to find these letter combinations in the story and read the words. Your child might find these words tricky:

asked   oh

Say these words for your child if they do not know them.

- Before you begin, ask your child to read the title to you by sounding out and blending. Talk about what the story might be about. What do they think Jack will find at the top of the beanstalk?

- Encourage your child to read the story to you. Talk about the pictures as you read.

- Your child will be able to read most of the words in the story, but if they struggle with a word, remind them to say the sounds in the word from left to right. Ask them to point to the sounds as they say them, and then blend the sounds into a whole word, e.g. b-ea-n.

- After you have read the story, look through it again and talk about it. Ask your child if they would rather have three gold coins, a hen that lays golden eggs, or a harp, and why.

- Do the 'Retell the story' activity together!

Jack and the Beanstalk

Written by Gill Munton

Illustrated by Constanze von Kitzing

OXFORD

UNIVERSITY PRESS

Jack and his mum had a cow.
Each day, Jack took a jug of the cow's milk to market.

Moo!

One day, there was no milk!
"Let's sell the cow," said Jack's mum.
"Then we can get some food."

Jack and the cow set off to market.
They met an old man.

"Will you sell me your cow?" he asked. "I'll pay you five beans."

"All right," said Jack.

When he got home, Jack's mum threw the beans away!
"Oh, Jack!" she cried. "What use are beans?"

The next day, one bean had grown into a huge beanstalk! Jack climbed up it.

13

At the top, he saw a giantess!
"You look hungry," she said. "I will
bake some bread."

Clink!

The giant had lots of gold coins.
He started to count them.

The giant fell asleep.

Zzz

Jack crept out of the chest and grabbed three gold coins. Then he ran home.

The next day, Jack climbed up the beanstalk again.
"You look hungry!" said the giantess.
"I will cook a pie."

But then...

Fee-fi-fo-fum!
Can I smell a boy?

"It's the giant! Quick, hide!"
said the giantess.

Squawk!

The giant had a hen.
She laid golden eggs!

The giant
fell asleep.

Jack crept out
of the pot and
grabbed the hen.
Then he ran home.

Zzz

21

The next day, Jack climbed up
the beanstalk for the third time.

"You look hungry!"
said the giantess.
"I will make a cake."

Plink!

The giant had a golden harp.
He started to play it.

Then he fell asleep.

Jack crept out of the box
and grabbed the harp.

Zzz

Plink!

The giant woke up!
"Come back!" he shouted.

Jack ran down the beanstalk.
The giant followed him!

But Jack's mum stood at the bottom with an axe! She chopped down the beanstalk.

So that was the end of the beanstalk, and Jack and his mum had all the food they needed!

Encourage your child to retell the story in their own words using the pictures as prompts. You could do this together, or take it in turns. Have fun!

Once upon a time...

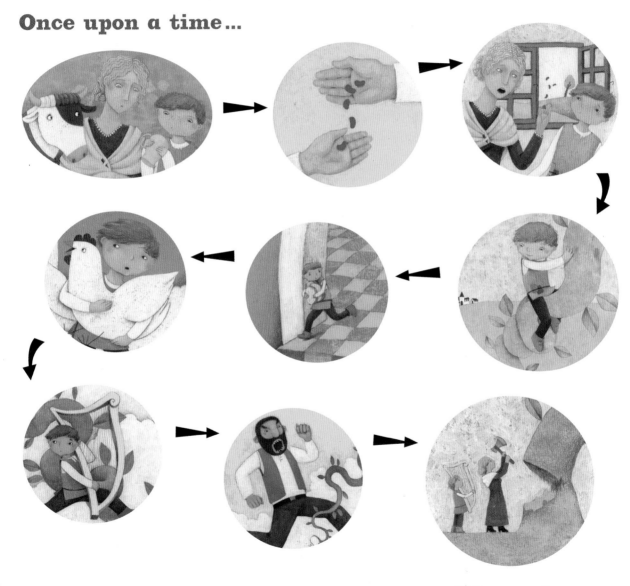

30

The end.

Tips for reading The Moon in the Pond together

About the story

This story is one of many tales about Brer Rabbit, a trickster.

This book practises these sounds:

ear (as in 'bear')   **ay** (as in 'way')   **e** (as in 'we')   **o** (as in 'told')

Ask your child to find these letter combinations in the story and read the words. Your child might find these words tricky:

their   asked   oh   called

Say these words for your child if they do not know them.

- Before you begin, ask your child to read the title to you by sounding out and blending. Talk about what the story might be about. Ask what they would usually expect to find in a pond.

- Encourage your child to read the story to you. Talk about the pictures as you read.

- Your child will be able to read most of the words in the story, but if they struggle with a word, remind them to say the sounds in the word from left to right. Ask them to point to the sounds as they say them, and then blend the sounds into a whole word, e.g. m-oo-n.

- After you have read the story, look through it again and talk about it. Would they like to have a friend like Rabbit. Why?

- Do the 'Retell the story' activity together!

The Moon in the Pond

Written by Chris Powling

Illustrated by Jeannie Winston

OXFORD
UNIVERSITY PRESS

It was night time. Rabbit, Fox and Bear were sitting by a deep pond.

"Shall we go fishing?"
said Rabbit.

"Fishing?" said Fox.
"In the dark?" said
Bear.
"Look at the moon,"
said Rabbit.

The moon was so big
and so round it lit up
the pond like daytime.

"See?" said Rabbit.
"We can fish till the
sun comes up."

37

Fox and Bear agreed. Rabbit grinned as they all went to fetch their fishing stuff, but he hid the grin with his paw.

He was playing a trick
on Fox and Bear.

Soon they were back at the
pond. Now they had rods
and lines and a big, big net.

"Let's start!" said Fox and Bear.

"Wait!" Rabbit yelped. "Look! I can see the moon in the pond! It must have dropped out of the sky."

"Is it sinking?" Fox asked.
"Will it drown?" asked Bear.
"Not if we save it," said Rabbit.

43

So they fished and fished
and fished.

Yet the moon still gleamed
in the pond.

"We must use our big, big net," said Rabbit at last.

"If I stay on the bank I can show you where to dip. You two must get in the pond close to the moon," he told them.

47

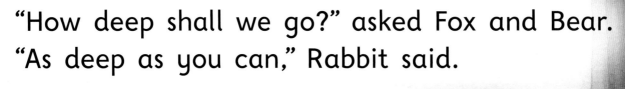

"How deep shall we go?" asked Fox and Bear.
"As deep as you can," Rabbit said.

Fox and Bear splashed into the pond. They flung the net this way and that.

Soon they were soaked from top to toe.
But they still did not save the moon.

"I'm wet all over!" Fox
yelled.
"I'm cold all over!"
added Bear.
"Oh dear ..." Rabbit said.

He jabbed his paw at the sky.
"The moon was up there all along.
It was not in the pond at all."

"ATCHOO!" sneezed Fox and Bear loudly.
"Sorry!" Rabbit called out.

Yet he was not sorry at all. Not when his trick had worked so well.

Rabbit was still grinning when the sun came up and Fox and Bear were still sneezing and cross.

Retell the story

Encourage your child to retell the story in their own words using the pictures as prompts. You could do this together, or take it in turns. Have fun!

Once upon a time...

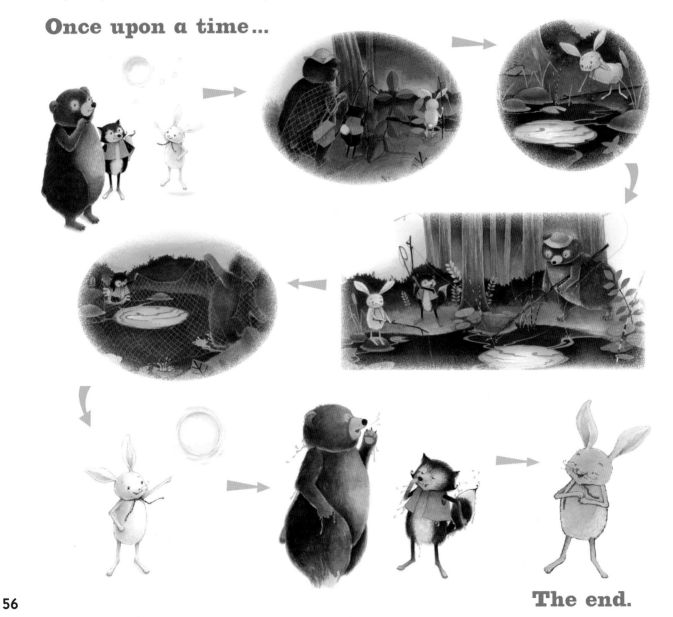

The end.

Tips for reading The Magic Paintbrush together

About the story

This story is based on a very old Chinese folk tale.

This book practises these sounds:

a–e (as in 'gave')   **ea** (as in 'real')   **o** (as in 'old')

Ask your child to find these letter combinations in the story and read the words. Your child might find these words tricky:

made   looked   people

Say these words for your child if they do not know them.

- Before you begin, ask your child to read the title to you by sounding out and blending. Talk about what the story might be about. Ask what a magic paintbrush might be able to do.

- Encourage your child to read the story to you. Talk about the pictures as you read.

- Your child will be able to read most of the words in the story, but if they struggle with a word, remind them to say the sounds in the word from left to right. Ask them to point to the sounds as they say them, and then blend the sounds into a whole word, e.g. j-ai-l.

- After you have read the story, look through it again and talk about it. Ask your child to find three or four kind things that Ho did to help others.

- Do the 'Retell the story' activity together!

Watch this story being performed by a professional storyteller on www.oxfordowl.co.uk

The Magic Paintbrush

Written by Liz Miles

Illustrated by Meilo So

OXFORD
UNIVERSITY PRESS

Every day, Ho looked
after a rich farmer's
cattle. He took hay
to the field.

The farmer did not pay him much. Ho had only dry bread to eat.

One day a very thin, old man came up the lane. He looked hungry. Ho gave his bread to the man.

"Thank you," said the man. He gave Ho a gift. It was a golden paintbrush.

63

Ho made paints
from plants, berries
and mud.

"What shall I paint?" thought Ho. He began to paint some hay. The hay became real!

This is a magic paintbrush!

The sun was hot. The stream was dry. So Ho painted a blue stream.

The stream became real! Now the people and the animals had water to drink.

The rich farmer had lots of food to eat.
But the children and workers were hungry.

Ho painted lots of food. It became real!

69

Ho painted lots of things for people.
They all became real. He painted ...

a wheel ...

a bucket ...

and some clothes.

The rich farmer
wanted the magic
paintbrush. He put
Ho in jail and took
the brush.

The farmer was greedy. He painted gold. But the gold did not become real.

"Oi, you! The paintbrush does not work for me. Paint me a mountain of gold!" ordered the farmer.

Ho painted the mountain of gold. He painted
a blue sea all around it. The gold and the
sea became real.

The farmer was angry.
"I cannot swim! Why did you paint
the sea?" he shouted.

"I will paint a ship for you," said Ho. The ship became real.

The farmer set off in the ship.
"When I get back, you will paint everything
I want. The world will be mine!" he laughed.

But Ho painted a gale. The gale became real. It took the farmer, far, far away.

Ho returned to the farm. He painted things
for those who were kind and good to others.

The rich farmer was
never seen again.

Retell the story

Encourage your child to retell the story in their own words using the pictures as prompts. You could do this together, or take it in turns. Have fun!

Once upon a time...

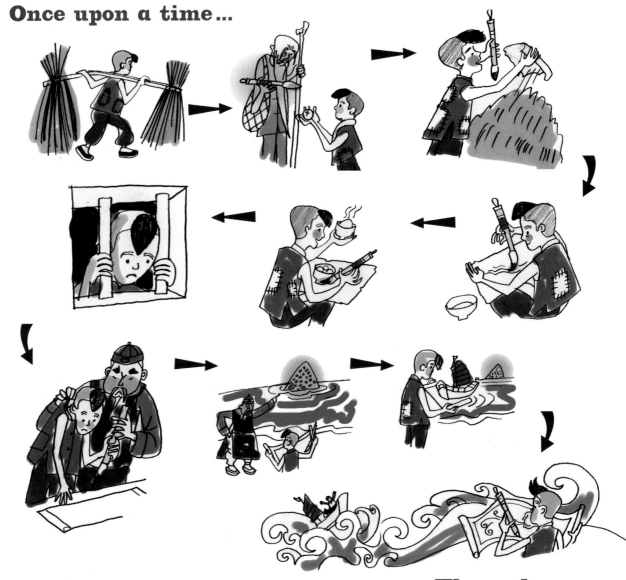

The end.

Tips for reading Oh, Jack! together

This story is based on an old English folk tale called 'Lazy Jack'.

This book practises these sounds:

a–e (as in 'cake')   **ay** (as in 'pay')   **y** (as in 'happy')

Ask your child to find these letter combinations in the story and read the words. Your child might find these words tricky:

called   oh   Mr   Mrs   people   looked

Say these words for your child if they do not know them.

- Before you begin, ask your child to read the title to you by sounding out and blending. Talk about what the story might be about. Ask what they think might happen to Jack.

- Encourage your child to read the story to you. Talk about the pictures as you read.

- Your child will be able to read most of the words in the story, but if they struggle with a word, remind them to say the sounds in the word from left to right. Ask them to point to the sounds as they say them, and then blend the sounds into a whole word, e.g. p-e-nn-y.

- After you have read the story, look through it again and talk about it. Ask your child if they think Jack's mum was happy at the end of the story.

- Do the 'Retell the story' activity together!

Oh, Jack!

Written by Jan Burchett and Sara Vogler

Illustrated by Teresa Murfin

OXFORD
UNIVERSITY PRESS

There was a boy called Jack. Jack sat about the house all day.

"Oh, Jack! Get a job," said his mum.

Jack got a job at the baker's shop.

Mr Brown the baker gave him a penny
for his pay, but he lost it.

"Oh, Jack! I'm very cross with you," said
his mum. "Put it in your pocket next time."

Jack got a job in the dairy.

Mrs Green the dairy owner gave him
a pot of milk for his pay.

On the way home he put it in his pocket.
The milk spilled onto the ground.

"Oh, Jack!" said his mum. "Put it on your head next time."

Jack got a job at the market.

Mr White the stallholder gave him
a cheese for his pay.

On the way home he put it on his head.
But the sun was very hot!
The cheese melted.

"Oh, Jack! What a mess," said his mum.
"Hold it in your hands next time."

Jack got a job with Miss Black the vet.

She gave him a cat for his pay.

On the way home he held it in his hands.
The cat got cross!

"Oh, Jack!" said his mum. "Put it on a lead next time."

Jack got a job at the cake shop.

Mr Grey the shopkeeper gave him
a cake for his pay.

On the way home he put it on a lead.

"Oh, Jack! You don't think," said his mum.
"Carry it on your shoulder next time."

Jack got a job on the farm.

Mrs Gold the farmer gave him a donkey for his pay.

On the way home he carried it on his shoulder. Lots of people saw him and chuckled.

Jack came by a big house.
A girl sat at the window.
She was very rich, but very sad.

She looked and saw Jack with the
donkey on his shoulder.
The girl giggled and giggled.

Jack made her happy.
They got married and lived happily
ever after.

Retell the story

Encourage your child to retell the story in their own words using the pictures as prompts. You could do this together, or take it in turns. Have fun!

Once upon a time...

The end.

Practise Your Phonics With

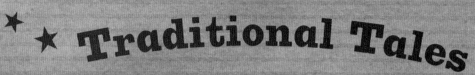
Traditional Tales

More stories for you to enjoy...

Practise Your Phonics With
Traditional Tales

The Gingerbread Man
and Other Stories

4 stories you can read by yourself!

OXFORD

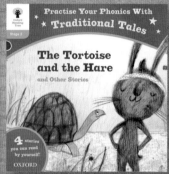

Practise Your Phonics With
Traditional Tales

The Tortoise and the Hare
and Other Stories

4 stories you can read by yourself!

OXFORD

Practise Your Phonics With
Traditional Tales

Chicken Licken
and Other Stories

4 stories you can read by yourself!

OXFORD

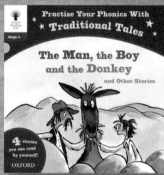

Practise Your Phonics With
Traditional Tales

The Man, the Boy and the Donkey
and Other Stories

4 stories you can read by yourself!

OXFORD

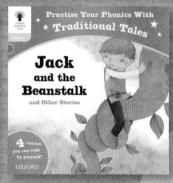

Practise Your Phonics With
Traditional Tales

Jack and the Beanstalk
and Other Stories

4 stories you can read by yourself!

OXFORD

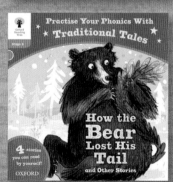

Practise Your Phonics With
Traditional Tales

How the Bear Lost His Tail
and Other Stories

4 stories you can read by yourself!

OXFORD

Help your child's learning with essential tips, phonics support and free eBooks

www.oxfordowl.co.uk

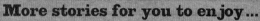